TURQUOISE

By Eric Ethan

Gareth Stevens
Publishing

Please visit our Web site, www.garethstevens.com. For a free color catalog of all our high-quality books, call toll free 1-800-542-2595 or fax 1-877-542-2596.

For Michelle, a real gem.

Library of Congress Cataloging-in-Publication Data

Ethan, Eric.
Turquoise / Eric Ethan.
    p. cm. — (Gems, nature's jewels)
Includes index.
ISBN 978-1-4339-4712-4 (pbk.)
ISBN 978-1-4339-4713-1 (6-pack)
ISBN 978-1-4339-4711-7 (lib. bdg.)
1. Turquoise—Juvenile literature. 2. Mineralogy—Juvenile literature. I. Title.
QE394.T8E74 2012
553.8'7—dc22

                                    2010030691

First Edition

Published in 2012 by
Gareth Stevens Publishing
111 East 14th Street, Suite 349
New York, NY 10003

Copyright © 2012 Gareth Stevens Publishing

Designer: Haley W. Harasymiw
Editor: Greg Roza

Photo credits: Cover, pp. 1, 5, 12, 13, 16, 17, 19, 21 Shutterstock.com; p. 7 Paul Chesley/National Geographic/Getty Images; p. 9 Scientifica/Visuals Unlimited/Getty Images; p. 11 Per-Anders/The Image Bank/Getty Images; p. 15 Joseph H. Bailey/ National Geographic/Getty Images; p. 20 Brand X Pictures/Getty Images.

Printed in the United States of America

CPSIA compliance information: Batch #CS11GS: For further information contact Gareth Stevens, New York, New York at 1-800-542-2595.

CONTENTS

Words in the glossary appear in **bold** type the first time they are used in the text.

What Is Turquoise?

Turquoise (TUHR-koyz) is a beautiful blue-green gemstone. It was one of the first gemstones ever mined. Silver and turquoise have been used in **jewelry** for thousands of years. Turquoise is a mineral. A mineral is a mix of different elements. Turquoise is a mix of the elements phosphorus, copper, and aluminum. Copper is what gives turquoise its blue-green color. **Polishing** turquoise until it shines is easy because the stone is so soft.

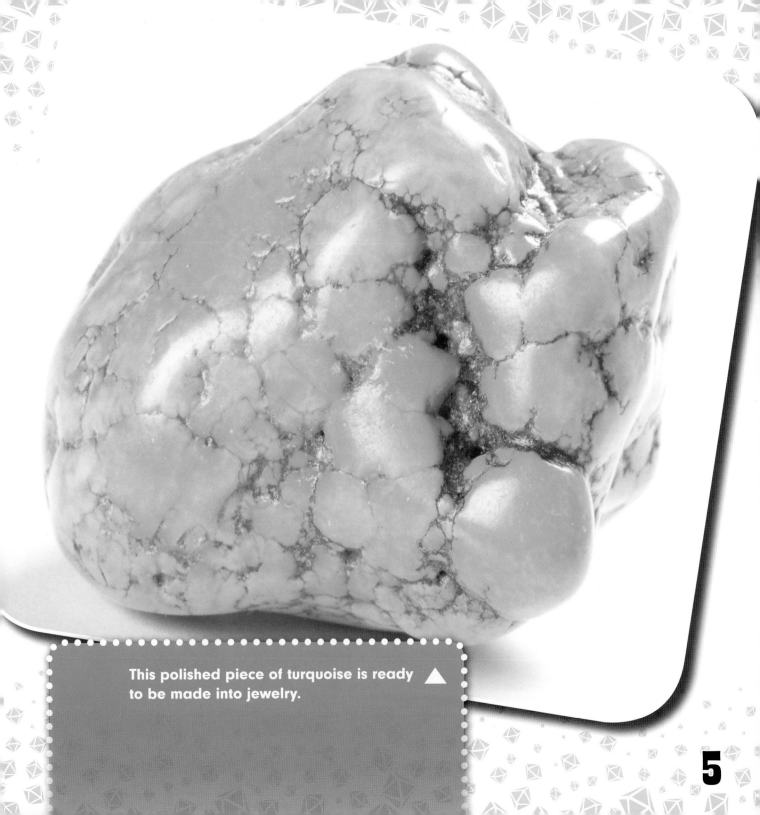

This polished piece of turquoise is ready ▲
to be made into jewelry.

Where Is Turquoise Found?

Turquoise was first mined in ancient Persia, which is today called Iran. Turquoise is one of the few gems mined **commercially** in North America. Mines in New Mexico are thought to have been active for over 1,000 years. Native Americans used stone tools to remove turquoise.

Nevada and Arizona are the largest producers of gem-**quality** turquoise in the United States. Nevada turquoise comes in several colors, including deep blue and bright green. One mine in Nevada has produced almost 400 tons since the 1870s.

GEM JOURNAL

Iran is still an important producer of turquoise.

Traditional Native American silver and turquoise jewelry is made from locally mined stone.

7

What Does Turquoise Look Like?

The most **valuable** turquoise is deep blue-green in color. It's sometimes called "robin's-egg blue" by people who sell turquoise jewelry. Even the best turquoise often has colors running through it that look like a spiderweb. Arizona turquoise often has a chocolate-brown web.

Turquoise has a soft, waxy appearance. Sometimes wax or oil is rubbed on turquoise stone when it's polished for jewelry. Doing this brings out the color of the stone and makes it look better.

This polished piece of turquoise shows a fine spiderweb of dark color.

At the Mine

Most turquoise is found close to the surface of the earth. **Deposits** are usually small. Small mines worked by a few people are common and produce most gem-quality turquoise. Miners use simple hand tools to dig for turquoise.

Because turquoise gets its blue-green color from the element copper, miners know that turquoise is only found in or near copper deposits. Sometimes copper miners and turquoise miners work together at the same mine.

GEM JOURNAL

Since turquoise deposits are usually small, it's uncommon for mining operations to include heavy machines.

A worker on a small copper mine washes stone from the mine. He may find turquoise mixed in with the copper.

11

Finding a Gem

Mining for turquoise is hard work. Only a small amount of gem-quality turquoise is found in most seams. A seam is a long, thin mineral deposit. Turquoise miners dig carefully as they look for signs of blue-green rock. Raw gem-quality turquoise doesn't look very much like jewelry.

This is a piece of raw turquoise and copper.

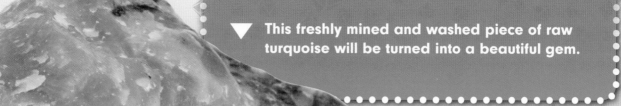

This freshly mined and washed piece of raw turquoise will be turned into a beautiful gem.

Miners remove the best-looking stone and wash it. This takes away the dirt and makes the raw stone shine. All the stone left after washing is sorted by the miners.

GEM JOURNAL

Most turquoise in a seam is not gem quality. Miners follow the seam hoping to find a small amount of really good stone.

Making Turquoise Jewelry

Turquoise chips easily. Jewelers must be very careful when they work with turquoise. They cut the gem-quality turquoise away from the other rock. Then they **grind** and polish the stone.

Turquoise from the southwestern United States is usually cut into thin, flat pieces. Then it's set on a flat piece of silver that has its edges turned up. This is called a bezel. It holds and guards the flat piece of turquoise.

GEM JOURNAL

The bigger the turquoise gem, the more valuable it is. Jewelers are very careful to keep the gem in one piece when cutting.

This Zuni Indian woman is wearing many pieces of thinly cut turquoise mounted in silver.

Treating Turquoise

Turquoise is a porous stone. This means it has tiny holes in it that can take in liquid. It's possible to dye light-colored turquoise a darker color to increase its value. Turquoise is sometimes treated to make it harder. A hard plastic coating is put over the outside of the gem. The coating keeps the stone from getting chipped or discolored.

The hardest kinds of turquoise are often made into beads for necklaces.

Turquoise from Iran is often harder than turquoise from other places. It can be made into beads and other carved shapes.

GEM JOURNAL

Turquoise beads have been worn as jewelry for thousands of years in the Middle East. It's often found there in ancient royal graves.

Valuable Turquoise

The most valuable turquoise is a deep-blue color. Large pieces that have no spiderwebs of other color in them are very **rare**. This makes them valuable.

A lot of the turquoise used in modern jewelry is treated. However, untreated turquoise is often worth more than treated turquoise. Very old silver and turquoise jewelry made by Native American craftsman in the southwestern United States has a special value all its own. It's usually made from large pieces of untreated turquoise.

This old silver jewelry contains very high-quality, untreated turquoise made by Native American craftsmen. ▲

19

Really Rare Turquoise

Turquoise isn't as highly valued as other gems, such as diamonds and emeralds. The most valuable turquoise is found in works made a long time ago. One of the most famous pieces was found in the **tomb** of the Egyptian king Tutankhamun. His gold mask contains **lapis** and turquoise. It may be the most famous turquoise piece in the world! Modern-day collectors pay many thousands of dollars for rare and beautiful Native American turquoise pieces.

King Tutankhamun's gold mask was discovered in 1922. It had remained buried for thousands of years.

Talking About Turquoise

- Turquoise is one of the birthstones for the month of December.

- Turquoise was often buried with Egyptian rulers because it was thought to keep them safe on their journey to the next world.

- Long ago, turquoise being taken to Europe passed through the country of Turkey. The word "turquoise" may have come from the old French word for "Turkey."

- Long ago, turquoise was thought to warn the wearer of danger by changing color.

- In ancient Persia, turquoise was believed to guard the wearer from evil.

- The very best turquoise in the world comes from the Sleeping Beauty mine in Arizona.

- Native Americans call turquoise "sky stone."

- Turquoise is the national stone of Iran.

Glossary

commercial: having to do with the buying and selling of goods and services

deposit: an amount of a mineral in the ground that built up over a period of time

grind: to shape or smooth something with a rough surface

jewelry: pieces of metal, often holding gems, that are worn on the body

lapis: a deep blue stone

polish: to make something smooth and shiny by rubbing it with a soft cloth

quality: the standard or grade of something

rare: uncommon or special

tomb: a burial room

valuable: worth a lot of money

For More Information

Books

Petersen, Christine. *Groovy Gems*. Edina, MN: ABDO Publishing, 2010.

Symes, R. F., and R. R. Harding. *Crystal and Gem*. New York, NY: DK Publishing, 2007.

Web Sites

The Dynamic Earth
www.mnh.si.edu/earth/text/index.html
Explore gems, minerals, and mining at the National Museum of Natural History Web site.

The Mineral and Gemstone Kingdom
www.minerals.net
Read about gems and minerals.

Turquoise Facts
www.turquoisefacts.com
Learn more about turquoise gems and mining.

Index